The Second Life of Bitcoin:

How Bitcoin and Blockchain are Changing the Economic World

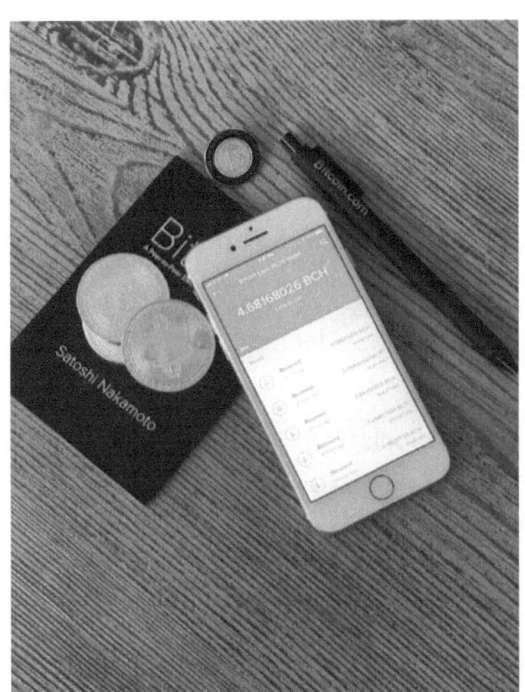

Copyright © 2018 b

All rights reserved.

The following eBook is reproduced below with the goal of providing information that is as accurate and reliable as possible. Regardless, purchasing this eBook can be seen as consent to the fact that both the publisher and the author of this book are in no way experts on the topics discussed within and that any recommendations or suggestions that are made herein are for entertainment purposes only. Professionals should be consulted as needed prior to undertaking any of the action endorsed herein.

This declaration is deemed fair and valid by both the American Bar Association and the Committee of Publishers Association and is legally binding throughout the United States.

Furthermore, the transmission, duplication or reproduction of any of the following work including specific information will be considered an illegal act irrespective of if it is done electronically or in print. This extends to creating a secondary or tertiary copy of the work or a recorded copy and is only allowed with an expressed written consent from the Publisher. All additional rights reserved.

The information in the following pages is broadly considered to be truthful and accurate account of facts, and as such any inattention, use or misuse of the information in question by the reader will render any resulting actions solely under their purview. There are no scenarios in which the publisher or the original author of this work can be in any fashion deemed liable for any hardship or damages that may befall them after undertaking information described herein.

Additionally, the information in the following pages is intended only for informational purposes and should thus be thought of as universal. As befitting its nature, it is presented without assurance regarding its prolonged validity or interim quality. Trademarks that are mentioned are done without written consent and can in no way be considered an endorsement from the trademark holder.

Table of Contents

Introduction 5
Chapter 1: Origins of Bitcoin 7
Chapter 2: Bitcoin and Blockchain – How it
 Works 18
Chapter 3: Pioneers of Bitcoin 29
Chapter 4: Other Cryptocurrencies 35
Chapter 5: Peaks and Valleys: Bitcoin Over the
 Years 47
Chapter 6: The Frontier: Bitcoin and the Future 58
Conclusion 69
Description 71
About the Author 73

Introduction

Bitcoin. Blockchain. Cryptocurrency. These are words we have all heard, but many of us are ignorant about what these words truly mean. The language of cryptography and computer programming is truly a foreign language, and much of the information about these key economic developments is rife with it. Many consumers find themselves between a rock and a hard place; they want to be able to get involved in something that seems to be a promising and innovative technology that is here to stay, but they can't find a resource that can explain the material simply!

In this book, we will provide an easy to understand explanation of the budding technology that lies behind Bitcoin and the reason this advance was so significant. We will put Bitcoin in perspective: looking at the advancements prior to it that made it possible, as well as the developments since then that continue to improve the technology of blockchain. We highlight well-known users and owners of bitcoins – some of which might surprise you! Bitcoin users are quite a diverse group.

We will also provide a brief look at some of the more popular and successful cryptocurrencies that are currently competing with Bitcoin. Despite over a thousand cryptocurrencies being developed in the last decade, Bitcoin continues to lead the pack. Bitcoin has a nuanced history despite its youth, and we will take you on a tour of some of the more dramatic moments and the growing pains it has experienced over the years. Finally, we will take a look at the predicted future of Bitcoin and whether or not it is here to stay.

Chapter 1:
Origins of Bitcoin

The beginnings of Bitcoin are shrouded in mystery. In 2008, a person or entity known only as Satoshi Nakamoto published a paper entitled "Bitcoin: A Peer-to-Peer Electronic Cash System." This paper not only outlined the perfect peer-to-peer system, it also provided exact specifications for putting the system into practice. Satoshi Nakamoto initiated the first block in his historic blockchain a few months later, and the rest is history. To this day, no one knows exactly who Satoshi Nakamoto is, although he has shared some limited personal information that has led to widespread speculation about his real-world identity. The fact that a person who created a highly influential currency that has shaped the past decade of the global economy is still unknown highlights one of the reasons that people enjoy cryptocurrency: anonymity. People who use cryptocurrency do not have to know each other or know who the person is outside of the virtual world, because cryptocurrency is not based on trust, it is based on math. To this day, trying to figure out the true identity of Satoshi Nakamoto is something of a sport in the cryptography community, with many theories abounding but no confirmation in sight.

Although it was not the intention of Satoshi Nakamoto, he would become the penultimate pioneer in the budding field of cryptocurrency. For years, people had been trying to find a way to create a viable cryptocurrency. A cryptocurrency is basically a digital currency that has no physical presence in the 'real world' – you couldn't take your 5 cryptocurrencies to a bank and get out anything that is physically tangible. The 'crypto' in cryptocurrency refers to the code that makes cryptocurrency workable. What makes cryptocurrency so complicated that it took this long for someone to put it into place? When making digital transactions, there is inherently an element of trust that you don't have in physical transactions. If you and I meet in the real world and I provide you currency for a good, you can see who I am, you can see the currency, and you can see that the currency is not being given to anyone else. While many virtual monetary transactions happen every day, most of these are done through what are considered to be trusted financial institutions that verify the parties and ensure currency is not used more than once. This is the 'double-spending' problem – how can you ensure that someone is not using a virtual currency more than once? We will talk about this more in a minute; right now, it is important that you know that until Satoshi Nakamoto, no one had been able to figure out a reliable way of solving the double-spending problem in a decentralized system, which was the ultimate obstacle to creating a reliable cryptocurrency.

To completely understand what makes cryptocurrency so significant, we must first understand how currency works in general. All currency only has meaning because of a general consensus that it has meaning and a trust in the system that backs the currency. If all Americans woke up tomorrow morning and as a group, decided that the American dollar no longer had any meaning and was not something they would accept as payment, the government (and banks) would be out of luck. Currency, such as dollars, is only a 'stand-in' for things that we want – this many dollars equals a car, this many dollars equals a house. In this way, cryptocurrency is similar to currency we are familiar with, as it is just a 'stand-in' for the tangible things that we want.

Most governments these days use what is known as a 'fiat money' system, in which the currency used does not actually have any intrinsic value but rather has value because the government says it does and the people agree to this. Alternatively, there are other currency systems known as 'commodity systems' in which the currency does have some kind of value outside of a government saying so. Gold would be an example of a currency in a commodity system that has some kind of inherent value. Another example that is common these days is cigarettes in the U.S. prison system. With a commodity system, the currency has value because it is something of use that most people in the system desire; with a fiat system, the currency has value because the government or interested parties agree that it has value and can be used to purchase goods.

Why are people interested in cryptocurrencies anyway? One of the reasons there has been so much consideration paid to creating cryptocurrencies is that these currencies are not overseen by any kind of regulatory authority such as a government or a bank. Economic crises and corruption in both banks and governments make it difficult at times to trust these systems with something as important as regulating currency, and this has created the drive to move away from a centralized system of currency and to create decentralized systems such as Bitcoin. The problem with decentralized systems – the problem that Mr. Nakamoto managed to solve and the reason why people favor regular currencies – is that it is exceptionally difficult with cryptocurrencies to ensure that someone does not 'double-spend' the currency in their possession, the problem we mentioned earlier. Let's say we are using a cryptocurrency called Leafs, and I agree to pay you 5 Leafs for a pizza. How can you make sure that I don't use those same 5 Leafs to pay for something else? How can you be sure I don't use those 5 Leafs to pay 10 different people? This is one of the benefits of using systems such as centralized banks – they are the arbitrator between parties who have such a problem or disagreement, as well as the regulator who identifies that you cannot use your 5 units of currency again once they've been given to someone else. They are considered 'trusted' institutions in that most people consider them to be relatively reliable and believe that the institution will act in good faith toward all parties involved. Satoshi Nakamoto solved this problem by making the ledger public so that any interested party could verify that users have the bitcoins they are spending.

Although Mr. Nakamoto is the one who was able to create a program that made cryptocurrency possible, he built on the work of many predecessors. David Chaum is a noteworthy cryptographer who preceded Mr. Nakamoto in trying to establish a feasible peer-to-peer cash system. Mr. Chaum accomplished this by using blind signatures, a cryptography process in which a 'message' is signed and verified without the signer 'reading' the contents of the message. This blind signature process led Mr. Chaum and his associates to develop a company they called Dig cash, in which currency could be traded with the financial institutions being 'blind' to the contents of the exchange. Mr. Chaum tried to engage with banks to help him with his new product, and this ultimately led to the downfall of his company, which declared bankruptcy in 1998. Anonymous sources from inside Dig cash maintain that David Chaum's poor management style and missed opportunities also contributed to the ultimate demise of the company.

Another currency innovator that laid the groundwork for Bitcoin were the founders of E-gold, established in 1996 right around the time that Dig cash was starting to fall apart. E-gold was based on users sending in valuable metals, such as gold and silver, and getting credit in the virtual realm for this – hence, 'E-gold.' E-gold enjoyed moderate success with over a million accounts at its peak. However, following the terrorist attacks of 9/11, the U.S. developed stricter laws for entities that facilitate money exchanges and ultimately targeted E-gold for prosecution. Ken Griffith, in an op-ed titled 'A Quick History of Cryptocurrencies BBTC – Before Bitcoin,' posited that the criminal element that had been attracted to E-gold is also what led to the government targeting it as a potential refuge of terrorists. Mr. Griffith notes that prior to 9/11, the

U.S. had policies that were generally encouraging to invention in the realm of digital currencies; in a post 9/11 world with anti-terrorist fervor at a fever pitch, these policies were reconsidered.

Mr. Nakamoto not only built on the foundation laid by previous attempts such as Dig cash and E-gold but also on the structure of chaining blocks that was developed by Stuart Haber and W. Scott Stornetta. These gentlemen worked on finding a way to make sure that a time-stamp on a digital document could not be tampered with, and it is this unalterable time stamp that is one of the core components of the blockchain used in Bitcoin. Their paper titled 'How to Time-Stamp a digital document', published in 1990, addressed the problem of how to ensure that someone cannot place a time/date stamp that is not the actual time/date, as well as how to ensure that someone cannot alter a digital time-stamp without the alteration being immediately apparent. This problem is one of the many difficulties that distinguish the virtual world from the physical world; in the 'real' world, one would be able to see markings indicating a change to a time-stamp or other signs of tampering. Haber and Stornetta wanted to create a way of denoting tampering in the virtual world that was comparable to the marks of tampering in the physical realm, and it was their work that allowed this to be incorporated into the original Bitcoin blockchain.

Perhaps the most significant predecessor to Bitcoin was computer engineer Wei Dai's theoretical 'b-money' system. Mr. Dai published a paper to a cypherpunk mailing list in 1998 which detailed a system extremely similar to Bitcoin; he addressed the double-spending problem by proposing each user keep their own ledger that is matched against all other ledgers in the system as a means of confirming transactions. In addition, the paper also proposed a 'proof-of-work' system similar to what Mr. Nakamoto eventually implemented in the Bitcoin system. Wei Dai did not intend to pursue implementing his b-money system and saw several flaws in his proposed system. Satoshi Nakamoto referenced Mr. Dai's paper in his initial white paper detailing the Bitcoin process; however, Mr. Dai has been asked multiple times about this and has stated that he believes that Mr. Nakamoto came up with the idea for Bitcoin independent of Mr. Dai's previous work. Whether or not Satoshi Nakamoto had read Mr. Dai's paper or not, the similarity between b-money and Bitcoin cannot be denied and at the very least primed a portion of the population to be receptive to a version that could be actually implemented.

The obscurity of Satoshi Nakamoto reflects one of the key foundations of Bitcoin, and by proxy, blockchain technology: there is no leader, there is no CEO, and there is no board that controls decisions. All decisions regarding Bitcoin software and the future of the cryptocurrency are made by majority; if the majority of computers or nodes running Bitcoin software support an update, the update is passed. Some people have concerns about Bitcoin because of the mysterious nature of Mr. Nakamoto; this concern reflects their ignorance of the core processes at the heart of blockchain. Mr. Nakamoto is the one who set the blockchain in motion and profited from the interest of others in Bitcoin, but his power ends there. In fact, many people speculate that the motivation behind the person or persons Mr. Nakamoto represents was not greed or personal power and that the money made from this venture represents a happy accident as opposed to the original goal. Many in the cryptography community have libertarian leanings and value privacy above everything; it was the pursuit of these values that led Satoshi Nakamoto to create Bitcoin. Establishing a decentralized currency exchange system is as good a way as any to throw off the yoke of governmental oversight and using cryptography in the system helps ensure the privacy of users. Whatever his, her, or their reasons for creating Bitcoin, Satoshi Nakamoto forever changed the economic world.

Chapter 2: Bitcoin and Blockchain – How it Works

Before we get deep into the technical processes behind Bitcoin, we do need to clarify one grammatical technicality. Bitcoin, when begun with an uppercase 'B,' refers to the software that the currency is based on, as in "They just released a new update for Bitcoin" or "I downloaded Bitcoin, and I've started mining." Bitcoin, when used with a lowercase 'b', refers to the actual currency, as in "I just made 5 bitcoins mining" or "Did you hear that one bitcoin is worth over $6,000?" In addition, one bitcoin can be broken down into increments of one million, which are called bits. This breakdown has become useful over the lifespan of the currency as the cost of one bitcoin has at times skyrocketed. Now, we will examine the blockchain, which is the cornerstone of Bitcoin and most cryptocurrencies in existence today. The blockchain is an incredibly innovative technology that many people are finding uses for outside of cryptocurrency.

Blockchain is the answer Mr. Nakamoto came up with for the question of how to prevent double-spending in online trans-actions. What if, instead of a financial institution holding the ledger, every user or purchaser were able to have access to the ledger? If everyone were able to mutually verify the transaction, the need for trusted third parties would disappear. Each 'block' contains records of transactions that have occurred across the network and been confirmed. Every computer or node that has Bitcoin software downloaded and running is part of the confirmation process for transactions, verifying that the user who paid the bitcoins actually has them to spend and has not attempted to use them elsewhere. If the transaction is false, it will not be confirmed and will not be added to the blockchain. The blockchain itself is a combination of several things. One, a link back to the previous block in the chain to ensure continuity. Two, all of the transactions that are being added to the blockchain and have been confirmed by the majority of nodes, and three, a complex mathematical problem that the author of the block has solved and is attached as 'proof-of-work' and can be inspected by all other users.

With most cryptocurrencies, the identity of the users is hidden, but the transaction itself is logged into the ledger. Everyone with access to Bitcoin can inspect the ledger and verify that it is authentic, and it is this open agreement that allows for the decentralization that is at the center of Bitcoin. Transactions are completed through strict protocols that rely on complex mathematical calculations from the branch of math known as cryptography to maintain the integrity of the system. This is the essence of the blockchain: each set of transactions forms a new 'block' in the chain that all users can inspect for themselves. It is quite the opposite of the trust-based system with banks and institutions: this system works on mutual distrust (in that anyone can openly check out the transactions and confirm for themselves that it was valid). The public ledger that constitutes the blockchain is stored not in one single location on one single server, but instead is stored across a vast network of servers made up of the individual users of Bitcoin. Whenever a new block is added to the chain, it is confirmed by other nodes on the network.

So how are new blocks added to the blockchain? The answer is another innovation that Bitcoin brought to the virtual world – mining. No, this is not mining for gold or coal like you might have thought – this mining is for the privilege of discovering or building the next block in the blockchain. Mining is the work that users do to verify and confirm transactions and add new blocks to the blockchain. It is designed to be resource-intensive, in that it takes time, energy, and computing power. As a reward for doing the work of confirming transactions and creating new blocks in the blockchain, miners are rewarded with bitcoins, and this is the only way that new bitcoins are created. The mathematical puzzles that miners must solve can be inspected by everyone and are known as 'Proof-of-Work.' Mining in Bitcoin has created a system in which any user who is willing to invest resources could be rewarded, without having any official affiliation with the creators of the blockchain. It incentivized individuals to do the work that was necessary to make the system function, without bestowing power on any one individual or group of individuals. Everyone is familiar with trusted institutions where CEOs or boards of trustees have ultimate power and rarely pay the price when things go awry. Mining does away with this hierarchical system and creates an egalitarian system in which anyone who wants to download the Bitcoin software and devote their computer resources to mining can help create the blockchain and profit from doing this work.

Who can become a Bitcoin miner? Anyone! It requires special hardware, but there are no limitations on who can purchase this and who can download the Bitcoin software. Mining is extremely competitive, and this can lead to purchasing increasingly powerful hardware to facilitate the process. Miners compete to solve mathematical proofs that will grant them the privilege of adding the next new block to the blockchain. This competition helps to maintain the democratic nature of Bitcoin, as it is extremely unlikely that one single miner would ever be adding consecutive blocks to the blockchain. The only way to discover the solution to the mathematical puzzles is by running thousands of calculations, so it is at random that a miner discovers the solution. However, once a miner discovers the solution and is granted the privilege of adding the next block to the blockchain (and collecting the bitcoins as a reward), it is very easy for other miners or users of Bitcoin to check their work and verify that the solution is legitimate. This confirmation of the work is one of the reasons that blockchain works.

Bitcoin software was the first instant of the use of blockchain, and since that time other cryptocurrencies have built on this foundation and are also using blockchain. Each blockchain is programmed with code that delineates the average amount of time to create a block. The creator of Bitcoin wrote into the Bitcoin code that the average amount of time to create a block in the blockchain should be 10 minutes. Other cryptocurrencies have smaller windows – Ethereum, a cryptocurrency founded in 2015, has an average block creation time of 14-15 seconds. To ensure that this window is maintained, the actual rate of block creation is assessed after a certain number of blocks are created. If the blocks are being created faster than 10 minutes, the program corrects this by increasing the difficulty of the mathematical puzzles needed for Proof-of-Work, thereby lengthening the amount of time for block creation. Conversely, if blocks are taking longer to create than the desired 10 minutes, the program will decrease the difficulty.

Just as blocks must be confirmed by other users and nodes to be added to the blockchain, updates, and changes to the Bitcoin software are also passed by democratic majority. In any blockchain, if there is significant dissension and a sizable portion of users would not confirm a decision, this would lead to what is known as a 'hard fork' in the blockchain. This kind of disagreement is rare in cryptocurrencies, but not unheard of; users sometimes have disagreements about the rules of the system which can lead to a hard fork. Bitcoin itself experienced a hard fork in 2017. The code of Bitcoin was originally created to limit the amount of all bitcoin transactions.

The foundation of the 2014 hack was a so-called 'bug' in the Bitcoin software that allowed the double-spending that blockchain was supposed to solve – skilled hackers were able to make it seem as though bitcoins had not been spent when in fact they had been. The exact nature of the problems inside the Mt. Gox exchange are still unknown, but documents leaked from inside the company make it seem as though someone may have been embezzling bitcoins from the exchange. Whatever the cause might have been, later that same month after the initial report of the hack Mt. Gox declared bankruptcy and thousands of people were left with empty pockets. The overall price of Bitcoin took a predictable nosedive. This safeguard was to keep spam and malicious users from overpowering the system. However, as Bitcoin grew, a divide in the community of users also grew: should the limit stay in place or should it be raised to accommodate the growth of the currency? The hard fork in 2017 was the result of the disagreement between these two camps. Bitcoin Classic stayed with the original one megabyte per ten minutes limit, while the new Bitcoin Cash increased the limit to eight megabytes. The split was handled graciously, as all who had bitcoins were given the same amount of Bitcoin Cash as they had in Bitcoin Classic, and given the choice to choose one or the other or to stick with having both. At present, Bitcoin Classic is still the leading cryptocurrency in terms of market value, with Bitcoin Cash coming in at 4th in the global cryptocurrency market.

One of the benefits of having a public ledger that is distributed across thousands of nodes is that it is generally considered to be difficult to hack, as opposed to a ledger that is stored on a single server and could easily be hacked and altered. In theory, if one node of the network is hacked and altered, it would be immediately obvious as the node's blocks would not match up with the rest of the networks, and mutual consensus would be that that particular node had been altered and was no longer valid. Bitcoin works through majority rule – the majority of the computers or nodes on the network must agree with something before it is accepted. There is no one ruler, one CEO, one individual or entity that makes decisions. If an update to the Bitcoin software is proposed, it must be accepted by the majority to be implemented.

Cryptocurrencies are able to hide the identity of the user by providing the user with an address that corresponds to their virtual wallet. Of course, once transactions have been made, there is always the possibility of a skilled hacker determining someone's identity by tracing patterns; but Bitcoin enthusiasts are constantly working on improving privacy as this is a primary concern within this community. The privacy concerns with Bitcoin have actually led to the development of several other currencies that we will explore later in the book.

How do people keep track of and store their cryptocurrency? Most people use virtual wallets, of which there are many different options to choose from. It is important to remember when choosing a wallet that you must keep it secure using a passcode, or in Bitcoin lingo, your 'private key.' As in the real world, if someone has your wallet (and the private key to get into it), they can take your cryptocurrency. Additionally, if you lose your private key and are unable to access your wallet, the currency is lost to you, and you will not be able to retrieve it and spend it. There are many anecdotal accounts of Bitcoin users who misplaced their private key that allowed them to access their Bitcoins and are now unable to reach the fortune they have amassed! Some desperate users, typically those who invested early and now would have a significant sum to their name, have even resorted to hypnotherapy to help them remember the lost key. While these stories are somewhat amusing, it is also a somewhat painful reminder that keeping your private key or passcode to access your Bitcoin wallet somewhere you can find it is VERY IMPORTANT.

There is hardware available that only functions as a Bitcoin wallet with no other purpose, such as TREZOR. These devices are the most secure and would be appropriate for someone who is storing a large amount of bitcoins. For casual users of bitcoins, web wallets that run on a website or application on your smartphone can be easier to access and more convenient. There is also the option to use coin exchanges on the web to store cryptocurrency; however, it is important to note that doing this is similar to storing money in a bank. Similar to banks, exchanges have been hacked and drained in the past, which makes some users wary of storing their currency there. All of the options have both upsides and downsides; before choosing, consider what you will be using your bitcoins for and whether the risk of potentially losing your coins is worth the ease of using an online exchange.

Chapter 3:
Pioneers of Bitcoin

Bitcoin and other cryptocurrencies make for odd bedfellows; from congressmen to libertarians, to cypherpunks, there's a wide assortment of individuals who are getting in on the cryptocurrency action. Some invest in Bitcoin in hopes to make money quickly; others see it as the future of the financial market; still, others are invested in the principles behind the blockchain itself. Still, others start using these currencies solely as a tool to achieve other goals, such as easy travel (or easy illegal activities, depending on the cryptocurrency you've chosen).

Recently, Congress revised their require-ments for disclosures of holdings to include that members disclose any cryptocurrency holdings. Interestingly, Representative Bob Good latte from Virginia disclosed that he has invested in several cryptocurrencies, including Bitcoin. He has connections to cryptocurrency as his son is an investor in the online cryptocurrency exchange known as Coin base. It seems to be a pattern that older generations are mostly connected to these new currencies through younger family members that have gotten involved in this new financial market. Although Rep. Goodlatte has remained silent about his personal investments in the world of cryptocurrency, other members of Congress have been vocal about their support for the young movement.

The chairman of the U.S. Commodities and Futures Trading Commission, J. Christopher Giancarlo, surprised everyone in early 2018 when he shared with a Senate committee that he sees the potential of Bitcoin and other cryptocurrencies. He shared openly that he had struggled to get his millennial children interested in the stock market despite much encouragement, and that it was finally the rise of Bitcoin that seemed to pique the interest he had so desperately been seeking. While advising caution as well as regulations to protect consumers, he seemed to indicate that he sees the cryptocurrencies as a currency of the future. He stated, "We owe it to this new generation to respect their enthusiasm about virtual currencies with a thoughtful and balanced response, not a dismissive one." Although Rep. Good latte has stayed quiet about his Bitcoin holdings, his actions of investing with the cryptocurrency would seem to reflect that he shares some of Mr. Giancarlo's views.

Perhaps one of the most surprising entities that have profited from the rise of Bitcoin is the U.S. government. In 2013, when the Silk Road online marketplace was raided and shut down, the U.S. government seized the assets which included 144,000 bitcoins. When the government sold the bitcoins, they made a staggering profit of $48 million. The reason behind the massive amount of bitcoins seized is that the website Silk Road used Bitcoin exclusively as payment. The Silk Road was founded in 2011 and was well-known for several years as a portal for finding illicit drugs and services. Although Bitcoin was not originally meant for criminal enterprise, the pseudonymous nature of the transaction originators lends itself to this easily. Notably, newer cryptocurrencies are actually now favored by the criminal element due to privacy improvements, which we will discuss in the next chapter. After the 2013 raid of Silk Road, the U.S. government had the largest single wallet store of bitcoins at that time.

Some users of Bitcoin and other cryptocurrencies tend to have libertarian leanings, as they believe that personal autonomy and liberty is extremely important. It is easy to see the appeal of cryptocurrency from the perspective of someone who is wary of governmental overreach: the anonymity of the transactions and the lack of involvement with a third party fit nicely into their belief system. Even for those who are not particularly libertarian, the last decade has seen an increase in the appeal of a system that steps away from trusting governments and banks. Many countries have experienced economic problems over the past ten years, and it seems like every month a new story breaks about corruption or fraud within the large banking systems. The collapse of the U.S. housing market in the mid-2000s and the resulting recession sowed distrust that set the stage for many people to become interested once Bitcoin was launched.

Another group that has been drawn to Bitcoin and other cryptocurrencies is cryptographers and those associated with the Cypherpunk movement. Cypherpunk is a movement that has grown alongside the internet; its members are concerned first and foremost with maintaining the privacy of the individual in the sea of new technologies we are all awash in. Privacy, cypherpunks maintain, is the ability of the individual to regulate how information about them is distributed and used – it does not preclude the individual from making disclosures, but it does prevent other third-parties (think Facebook selling data about users) from disseminating information about the user. It is not surprising that the cypherpunk community would be interested in Bitcoin; not only is the principle behind Bitcoin and blockchain in line with the desire for privacy, but it was on a cypherpunk mailing list that Satoshi Nakamoto first published the white paper that became the basis for Bitcoin. Bitcoin has an almost cult-like following in these circles, as the main beliefs it stands for are completely in line with the values of the cypherpunk community. These individuals are not involved in Bitcoin for the profits but for the principles.

In terms of straight demographics, the statistics on Bitcoin users is mostly what you would expect. According to Coin Dance, a website that collects data about Bitcoin, its users, and other cryptocurrencies, the vast majority of Bitcoin users are male (over 90%), over 60% are between the ages of 18 and 34, with a little less than a quarter in the 35-44 age range. This is unsurprising, as younger generations have seemed more engaged with cryptocurrencies than older generations. Predictably, many of the people involved in Bitcoin are those interested in personal investing and technology; however, there is a small percentage that is involved in travel that is engaged with Bitcoin as well. The usefulness of Bitcoin in traveling is that, unlike with currencies such as the dollar or pound, you don't have to trade currency back and forth (and lose a percentage of it during this process), as bitcoins are the same everywhere you go.

Chapter 4: Other Cryptocurrencies

As a result of the revolutionary technology that Mr. Nakamoto introduced, hundreds of other cryptocurrencies have sprung into existence, with estimates that there are over 1500 different cryptocurrencies at this time. Some cryptocurrencies have emerged and then died as quickly as they were conceived; others have quickly moved up in popularity. Some are decentralized, as Bitcoin; others are more centralized. Some use the blockchain primarily as a platform for running other programs and only use cryptocurrency as a means of exchange in that program; others mimic Bitcoin in establishing a currency that can be used anywhere it is accepted. In short, Bitcoin has given rise to a hugely diverse number of cryptocurrencies! Here, we will review some of the more popular and successful cryptocurrencies that Bitcoin has helped to spawn.

What better place to start than with the Bitcoin/Bitcoin Cash split? As we mentioned earlier, Bitcoin experienced a hard fork in 2017 when users differed strongly about whether to increase the amount of data processed for each block, and this led to the creation of Bitcoin Cash. Unsurprisingly, Bitcoin Cash is a popular cryptocurrency, although it has not reached the level of popularity that its parent Bitcoin Classic has enjoyed. The major difference between the two cryptocurrencies is that Bitcoin maintains the one-megabyte block size, while Bitcoin Cash increased the size of blocks to eight megabytes, which allows blocks to be created faster. Interestingly, Bitcoin Cash is not the only split that Bitcoin has experienced – there have been several other hard forks in the history of Bitcoin, including initiation of 'Bitcoin Unlimited' and 'Bitcoin XT.' However, most of the other children of the hard forks have fallen out of favor and gradually faded into the background; Bitcoin Cash is the only child of Bitcoin that has shown the possibility of rivaling its parent.

Lite coin is another cryptocurrency which was founded in 2011 and is similar to Bitcoin in that it relies on blockchain; however, transactions on lite coin are generally faster than those on Bitcoin. Lite coin was one of the first cryptocurrencies to change the time it takes to create a block in the blockchain; lite coin averages 2.5 minutes to Bitcoin's 10 minutes, which makes it faster. Like Bitcoin, it has a big focus on decentralization, and some believe it to be simply a clone of Bitcoin. Initially, Lite coin had some updated features that set it apart from Bitcoin; as Bitcoin software is updated, however, some speculate that lite coin may become obsolete. Others predict that lite coin will continue to grow; currently, it is the 7th largest cryptocurrency in the world. While predictions for the future of lite coin are clearly mixed, it has lasted 7 years, which is practically an eternity in the world of cryptocurrency.

Ethereum is a popular cryptocurrency that was founded using the blockchain technology pioneered by Satoshi Nakamoto. Ethereum was founded by Vitalik Buterin, a young computer programmer who was involved with Bitcoin during its early days. Although it was only founded in 2015 and is thus relatively young compared to Bitcoin, Ethereum is the second largest cryptocurrency in the world at this time, and some experts believe that it will surpass Bitcoin soon. Vitalik Buterin saw the blockchain as a potential source of unsurpassed computing power that could be harnessed and put to good use rather than used solely for completing meaningless calculations. One of the innovations that Mr. Buterin came up with is running what are known as 'decentralized apps,' or applications that harness the processing power of the network to store information.

The cryptocurrency of the Ethereum network is 'ether,' however, cryptocurrency is hardly the only thing that Ethereum is known for, as its primary appeal was in being able to use blockchain technology to build decentralized apps as well as used for so-called 'smart contracts.' A smart contract is a computer protocol that enforces an agreement between users. Nick Szabo, a computer engineer, is credited with coming up with the idea for smart contracts in 1994, but the ability to actually put it into use was impossible until the blockchain technology that Bitcoin brought into the world. Interestingly, many people believe Nick Szabo to be the elusive Satoshi Nakamoto, despite multiple denials by Mr. Szabo. Many believe that the use of smart contracts in blockchain can be used to eliminate the need for trusted third parties who enforce contracts; in smart contracts, the agreement is written into the code of the blockchain and is witnessed by the thousands of other users. Smart contract enthusiasts maintain that this new technology could fundamentally change the way we make contracts and could cut out the middlemen of lawyers and other mediators.

One cryptocurrency that has been the subject of hot debate is Ripple, currently ranked as the 3rd largest in the world. Ripple was started in 2012 and was initially released with the intention of being a kind of 'go-between' currency, marketed as a way to send and receive currency quickly by using XRP (the token of the Ripple network). Its creators did not envision the currency itself having much value other than as a way of exchanging other currency; users of Ripple don't have to own any actual XRP to make exchanges using the software. The reason for the scrutiny of Ripple is that, unlike Bitcoin and other popular cryptocurrencies, it is not decentralized and does not use blockchain in the traditional sense of the word. Instead, it uses a system of trusted servers to confirm transactions and ensure consensus on the network. With Bitcoin and other cryptocurrencies, anyone can download the software and become a node on the network that assists in confirming the blockchain; with Ripple, only certain servers are allowed. As a result of this, mining is not needed for XRP, and an arbitrary number of XRP was released with the initiation of the software.

In contrast, Bitcoin is being slowly released through mining, culminating in a peak number that experts estimate won't be reached for decades. Ripple is useful for making exchanges between currency, but true crypto fanatics are skeptical of it and worry that it could be overtaken by large institutions such as banks. These skeptics point to the favorable relationships that Ripple has developed with these institutions to facilitate exchanges of currency quickly.

Zcash is a cryptocurrency similar to Bitcoin that was developed by Zooko Wilcox to address privacy concerns that some users had with the Bitcoin blockchain. While your identity is not transparent during Bitcoin transactions, the address that you use to make Bitcoin transactions might eventually be connected to you as the number of transactions accumulates and patterns begin to emerge. If your identity is compromised and revealed and attached to your Bitcoin address, it may be possible for information about you to be gathered from the public blockchain account of transactions, information such as your Bitcoin holdings and amount of currency you've paid to others. Mr. Wilcox proposed to solve this privacy issue by masking certain aspects of the transaction so that not every part of the transaction is transparent, while still ensuring that enough is visible that the transaction can be confirmed as valid. This masking of certain aspects of transactions also ensures that each unit of Zcash is equal to any other unit of Zcash; since the transaction history of each individual unit is unknown, users cannot discriminate when purchasing. This has not always been the case for bitcoins; since each bitcoin's history can be traced in the public blockchain, some users are willing to pay more for 'clean' bitcoins that are untarnished by particular addresses or transactions. Zcash was launched in 2016 and as of this writing ranks as the 20th largest cryptocurrency.

Dash, previously known as 'Dark coin,' was launched by Evan Duffield in January 2014, initially as a split from the previously discussed lite coin. Dash differs from Bitcoin in two primary ways: one, 10% of all currency mined is set aside to be used to improve the software and systems associated with the cryptocurrency. In this manner, it is a self-supporting system that does not rely on volunteers, unlike Bitcoin. The second main difference is that instead of having a large and diverse group of miners who are all treated equally, Dash has two levels of miners: regular miners and 'master nodes.' To become a master node, one must purchase 1000 Dash coins. The benefits of becoming a master node include a vote on what projects are backed by Dash and the ability to have private transactions. Some in the crypto community object to the tiered structure Dash has introduced, arguing that the Dash network cannot be considered to be truly decentralized when so much power rests in the hands of the master nodes. Despite such criticism, Dash currently comes in at 14th in the cryptocurrency market capitalization ratings.

Monero is the third cryptocurrency in the privacy-prizing triumvirate, along with Zcash and Dash. The seven developers of Monero, five of whom have remained anonymous, were similarly concerned as the founders of the two previous currencies about the potential for discovering a user's identity or learning other key information about users from the Bitcoin blockchain. Similarly to Zcash, the increased privacy of the Monero currency prevents users from favoring certain coins over others; one unit of Monero is equal to any other given unit of Monero, as users have no way of knowing if that unit might have been involved in illegal or other unsavory transactions previously. One of the ways that Monero achieves privacy on the blockchain is by using cryptography called 'ring signatures.' Basically, when you sign a transaction using Monero, and it is sent to the blockchain for processing, a number of 'decoys' are pulled at random from past blockchain transactions to prevent others from determining where the true signature came from. To prevent double-spending, the software uses another type of cryptography based on key images that allow miners to verify that the unique key image produced from the transaction has not been used before. Monero proudly claims that its transactions are completely anonymous and untraceable as a result of these unique features. Currently, Monero is coming in at 10th in terms of the size of cryptocurrency.

All forms of currency and units of exchange will attract criminal elements, and cryptocurrency is no exception. There does seem to be some preference among users who are engaging in illegal activities; recent research indicates that Monero, Zcash, and Dash are preferred cryptocurrencies for crime due to the increased privacy that they afford users. While this is certainly no fault of the currency itself, the fact that certain ones are more likely to be used by criminals does mean that law enforcement agencies and eventually governments may pay particular attention to these and perhaps more strictly regulate them. In April of this year, Japan moved to discourage coin exchanges from using the cryptocurrencies favored by the criminal element. So while there are currencies that afford more privacy than Bitcoin, this privacy comes at the cost of using a currency that may be more likely to be targeted by governments and law enforcement.

The tide of new cryptocurrencies shows no sign of slowing down. Blockchain technology truly unlocked a torrent of creativity in the realm of cryptography and computer programming, and a young and energetic generation has embraced it full throttle. When trying to decide on a cryptocurrency to invest in, it is probably best to do a fair amount of research before choosing one. Each cryptocurrency offers particular features at the cost of others. Many people choose a cryptocurrency that they find to be in line with their personal values; those who value decentralization wouldn't choose Ripple as their currency of choice, for example. Bitcoin is the obvious choice as it has been around the longest and continues to top the market despite its many competitors; an impressive feat considering the number of competitors has topped a thousand! Bitcoin has also weathered many storms, which we will examine in the next chapter.

Chapter 5:
Peaks and Valleys: Bitcoin Over the Years

Bitcoin has experienced numerous rises and falls as well as rather interesting episodes over almost ten years it has been in existence. Like any new technology, there were kinks to work out; one early kink was revealed in 2010 when Bitcoin was hacked and a major invalid transaction executed. When flaws are found in the Bitcoin software, new versions can be formulated and approved by users. As Bitcoin software is updated based on a majority vote from all Bitcoin users, there are times when some users do not support the update and choose instead to fork into their own cryptocurrency, as was the case with Bitcoin Cash.

In 2011, the darknet website Silk Road was launched, and Bitcoin was its currency of preference. The Silk Road was a website where users could purchase illicit drugs, forged documents, and other illegal goods, so using a cryptocurrency that somewhat limits traceability makes sense. For the next three years as the Silk Road prospered, Bitcoin was somewhat associated with the scandal of purchasing illicit goods. However, it is worth noting that there is nothing inherently illegal or illicit in using Bitcoin or any other cryptocurrency; it was not designed for this purpose, but criminal elements saw the potential for use.

Unfortunately for Silk Road founder Roger Ulbricht, the government was highly motivated to shut down the darknet exchange and succeeded just a few years after it was launched. After Silk Road was shut down and other more private cryptocurrencies were developed, Bitcoin began to shed some of this scandalous reputation. Interestingly, some people speculate that users who bought goods from Silk Road could be troubled by these transactions at some point in the future, as researchers have discovered that due to the public nature of Bitcoin's blockchain it may be easy for law enforcement agencies to track purchases made on the Silk Road. This factor also contributed to the criminal element moving to more private cryptocurrencies such as Monero.

The first bitcoin 'block' in the blockchain was mined by Satoshi Nakamoto on January 3, 2009, just a few months after Mr. Nakamoto published the white paper introducing the idea of Bitcoin to the world. Known as the Genesis block, this block is the one that started it all and is irrevocably tied to all future blocks on the Bitcoin blockchain. There are now thousands of blocks the Bitcoin blockchain. Almost a year and a half later, in May of 2010, the first real-world purchase was made using Bitcoin – 10,000 bitcoins for two Papa John's pizzas. With the current exchange rate between bitcoins and dollars, that would be $60 million for two pizzas! However, without this initial foray into using bitcoins to pay for real-world items, it is unlikely Bitcoin would have grown as much as it has. In February of 2011, one bitcoin became equal to one dollar, a huge achievement for the young currency. Early 2011 was mostly a good year for Bitcoin, as it began to receive more attention from the mainstream media, and also surpassed parity with the Euro.

Interest grew in Bitcoin after the fall of the U.S. economy, but in June 2011 the first big hack of

Bitcoin sent people running in fear that cryptocurrency may not be the savior of economies that they were hoping for. The rush to sell bitcoin drove the price down, and many speculated that Bitcoin would be short-lived. However, Bitcoin proved more resilient than the skeptics thought. Confidence began to increase in the young cryptocurrency, and the price of bitcoins again began to rise steadily. Many young entrepreneurs, seeing an opportunity, launched exchanges where users could store their bitcoins and easily make transactions. The bitcoin exchange known as Mt. Gox, which was associated with the hack in 2011, was hacked in 2014 in a much larger fashion. At the time of the 2014 hack Mt. Gox was managing an estimated 70% of all bitcoin transactions.

Although many are wary of such a huge hack and massive loss of value as the 2014 Mt. Gox hack, the increased regulation and scrutiny of cryptocurrency exchanges makes it less likely that something of this scale could happen again. As of March 2018, the U.S. Securities and Exchange Commission began requiring that cryptocurrency exchanges register with them, providing a level of oversight not previously seen. This is somewhat ironic as one of the reasons for the popularity of Bitcoin is a move away from 'trusted' entities such as governments and banks; however, it is worth noting that this move is only to regulate the exchange and does not actually interfere with the Bitcoin process itself in any way. At the time the new regulations were announced, the SEC chairman Jay Clayton reassured major cryptocurrencies such as Bitcoin and Ethereum that the goal was to provide smart policies that did not overly hinder the processes of the currencies.

While in the process of announcing these new regulations, J. Christopher Giancarlo, chairman of the U.S. Commodities and Futures Trading Commission, shared with the committee that his children had finally become interested in the stock market as a result of Bitcoin and blockchain. He advised that it is important to take these new currencies seriously, calling them an innovation and praising their ability to interest the younger generation in financial markets. At the same time, he indicated that it is important for the committee to set in place regulations that protect consumers and investors from fraud. As the popularity of Bitcoin grows, statements such as these from well-respected politicians in the public eye will only contribute to people giving these currencies due consideration.

After the Mt. Gox 2014 hack and loss of so many bitcoins, the value of bitcoin declined, and Bitcoin had a hard two years trying to recover from the staggering blow. Many Bitcoin users had been trusting exchanges to store their currency safely, and the fiasco in 2014 served as a harsh reminder that one of the primary reasons for using Bitcoin in the first place was the decentralized nature. Bitcoin exchanges provide the ease of banks, but also have the downsides of banks – namely, that someone might steal all your money. As most coin exchanges are relatively new since cryptocurrencies are young, users take a risk by trusting that the exchange is going to behave in good faith and store their currency in a secure manner. Undoubtedly, users who suffered through the aftermath of 2014 became much more cautious before trusting their bitcoins to third-party exchanges.

2014 was not all bad for Bitcoin – the end of the year saw Microsoft begin taking payments in bitcoins. A spokesperson for Microsoft indicated that they saw the cryptocurrency as something that would be around long enough for them to begin using it as a currency. The year before the Mt. Gox fiasco Bitcoin had been recognized both in the United States and in Germany as a form of currency. As Bitcoin became more recognized, more and more retailers started working on accepting it as a form of payment. It is estimated that there have been about forty major thefts in Bitcoin history, and it is worth noting that most of the thefts have occurred as a result of a flaw in the security of coin exchanges, not flaws in the Bitcoin software itself. Many people rely on coin exchanges as a means of storing and accessing their bitcoins and while this is convenient, using an exchange is a risk.

Proponents of cryptocurrencies would argue that paper currency is rapidly becoming outdated and that the world of virtual currencies can be made much more secure through blockchain. They even argue that using Bitcoin and other software such as it could result in an overall decrease in crime, as paper money in the real world is frequently both the focus of crime and the intermediary in crime.

Bank robberies are a prime example of a crime that only exists because of paper currency. Paper currency, typically issued by the government, is also subject to the government's whims. Several significant events in Bitcoin's history are related to world governments engaging in risky financial behavior and driving their citizens into the arms of the relatively more secure cryptocurrency.

This problem with unfavorable financial decisions was illustrated in India in 2016 when the government issued a declaration that two of the primary paper notes in circulation (making up 86% of the existing paper currency) was no longer going to valid as a method of payment. While the target of this declaration was tax evasion and the rationale behind it was not malicious, finding out that most of your paper currency is worthless is jarring for anyone (unsurprisingly), and this announcement caused massive chaos in India. Those who favor systems like Bitcoin point to incidents such as this as proof that we would all be better off using impartial and decentralized currency systems where no one person could up-end the system through rash proclamations. Undoub-tedly, moves by governments such as the one in India in 2016 have helped to drive up the popularity and success of Bitcoin.

It is foreseeable, then, that Bitcoin and other cryptocurrencies are more likely to become popular in nations that are in turmoil and that have lost faith in the third-party institutions they are supposed to be able to trust. As we discussed earlier, trust is absolutely essential for governments and banks to be able to function – without trust, the system falls apart. In many countries, corruption and other negative forces have made the government into an entity that truly cannot be trusted –

and it is in these places that people are more willing to give Bitcoin a try. Venezuela is a prime example of this – inflation in 2017 was off the charts, and the people became desperate as the government tried to fix the problem by printing more and more money. Bitcoin mining became a popular means of earning the currency to get much-needed supplies, as well as a way to send and receive currency across the world. Effective bitcoin mining relies on electricity, and this is a resource that Venezuelans do have access to. Unfortunately, there is some indication that Venezuelan police began seizing mining equipment on bogus charges and using the mining equipment for themselves.

Particular countries aside, Bitcoin experienced a massive resurgence in 2017 which was the best year to date for the currency. By 2017, other cryptocurrencies had been established and were coming into vogue, fueling the drive to invest in this new technology. Although there are many different cryptocurrencies to choose from, many people have only ever heard of Bitcoin and chose it as their preferred virtual currency. 2017 was also the year that Bitcoin experienced a hard fork and Bitcoin Cash was born and quickly rose in popularity. The start of 2018 has seen some ups and downs in the currency, as Bitcoin rose to being worth almost $10,000 per coin but has since lowered to being worth about $6,000 at present. A popular meme in cryptocurrency circles is an image of the Bitcoin logo riding a rollercoaster – on days it spikes, the rollercoaster is shown going up; on days it plummets, the rollercoaster is shown speeding down. This fun illustration is a reminder that it is to be expected that this young currency will experience drastic rises and falls, but that overall its growth is moving in an upward direction. In the next chapter, we will examine where Bitcoin is headed in the future.

Chapter 6:
The Frontier: Bitcoin and the Future

Since public trust and investment in currency is truly the only way for a currency to grow and thrive, this will be an important factor in determining the future of Bitcoin. One aspect of this is the reaction that various countries and governments have had (and are having, as this is continuing) to Bitcoin and other cryptocurrencies. Countries have had mixed reactions to Bitcoin. Some countries, such as Thailand and China, have outright banned it and do not permit it to be used in their country. Other countries have embraced it, such as Canada, who founded one of the first 'bitcoin ATMs.' In the early 2010s, some companies foresaw the growth of Bitcoin and began accepting it as payment, such as Microsoft. Japan, always on the lookout for growing technological trends, began recognizing Bitcoin in 2017. Now, there are over 1000 bitcoin ATMs worldwide, showing the overall growth of the founding cryptocurrency. Several countries in Europe, as well as Australia, Canada, the United States, and Chile, have reacted favorably to Bitcoin and actively encouraged its use. Overall, most countries have not reacted in the extreme negative fashion of China, and are either favorable or neutral to cryptocurrencies.

Some people are reluctant to get involved with Bitcoin and other cryptocurrencies because of a misconception that these virtual currencies are involved with fraud and criminal enterprises. While there have been cases where these currencies are connected to criminal dealings, it is through no fault of their own, nor any particular aspect of virtual currencies. Any currency, any unit of exchange, be it the dollar or the pound or the bitcoin, will attract its share of the criminal element – this is just a universal truth. As long as there has been a system of money or exchange in place, there have been people who have tried to game or cheat the system. In ancient times, when the currency was a weight of barley or a weight of silver, some people would try to alter the scales or the metals to cheat others. This impulse is as old as time itself and is nothing special or unique to virtual currencies; rather, it gets more attention when it happens with Bitcoin because of the novelty of cryptocurrencies. Everyone is well aware that cash money is well-used by criminal elements in our society, so much so that attempting to make more cash through counterfeiting is a constant problem that the U.S. government is pursuing. We don't hear stories about this often, though, because it's nothing new and the dollar is not gathering attention like the bitcoin. So when you read stories about Bitcoin and other cryptocurrencies being the target of fraud or other scandals, remember that this is nothing unique to Bitcoin.

Virtual currencies may seem strange, but in reality, much of the dealings that we do in this day and age involves similar exchanges. There are many people these days that rarely have cash or rarely touch cash. You can go months with only using 'virtual' dollars to pay for things. Say you get paid through direct deposit into your bank account – your company sends the information through a trusted institution, and the numbers show up in your account. You haven't actually touched any currency in the physical realm. Then you pay your bills – which you do online, the numbers moving out of your account and into the accounts of those you owe. Now, this system works because you trust that if for whatever reason you needed the physical money, your bank would provide it. You also trust your bank and the other institutions in the interactions to behave in good faith and not cheat you. However, if everyone in America suddenly decided that they wanted to hold all of their money in their hands, our society would collapse – because there isn't enough physical money to match the 'virtual' money we have represented in all of our collective bank accounts. The system works because we trust it and don't panic and withdraw all of our money. We've seen this collapse before – where customers panic and attempt to take out money. So really, cryptocurrency is not as radical as you might think – it is simply the next step in the natural evolution of currency.

Another potential reason that cryptocurrencies like the bitcoin could work is that the Bitcoin software is written to only allow a certain number of bitcoins to be created, culminating in a limited number that is capped. This scarcity prevents inflation from being an issue with Bitcoin. Many governments had made the mistake of printing more and more paper money to try to solve economic problems, leading to hyperinflation and days when paper money was only worth fuel for the fire. When the limit to the amount of cryptocurrency is written into the code, this kind of inflation and subsequent economic collapse is not possible. Not all cryptocurrencies have this built-in hard limit, although some do mimic Bitcoin in this regard.

Some other advantages of Bitcoin technology are clear: transactions are completed quickly, with little processing time compared to major financial institutions. The transactions are confirmed through consensus and miners dedicated to doing the work necessary to build the blockchain. Mining happens all day, every day – no breaks, no holidays. There are no mandatory transaction fees, such as those you might pay when you take cash out of an ATM that does not belong to your bank. However, some miners might elect to charge transaction fees in exchange for processing transactions faster. Typically, this is done based on how much energy the transaction will take to process. There is no transaction too small for Bitcoin software, and you are not charged a fee for making tiny transactions as you might be when making a small purchase at a store that has to pay fees for using credit cards. Bitcoin transactions, once confirmed and added to the blockchain, are generally seen as irreversible – it has been written into the code and cannot be altered or changed. The more blocks are added to the blockchain, the less chance that anyone can dispute the transaction. There is no higher authority to appeal to, no way that the transaction could be reneged on, which protects users from fraud. If someone pays you with bitcoins, it's because they have the bitcoins to pay you – no bounced checks in the blockchain. Anyone can inspect the blockchain and see the record of transactions made.

For anyone who has ever had a problem with a government or bank freezing their assets, Bitcoin is all the more appealing. With Bitcoin, no one has the power or control over the system to freeze your coins, so you are never in danger of a corrupt official using the system to hurt you. In some countries, this is a legitimate fear and makes the option of a decentralized currency very attractive.

Bitcoin also has the advantage of being mobile, meaning that wherever you take your virtual wallet, there you have your access to your money. The rising problem of identity theft has also made Bitcoin a tempting choice for some consumers. Many stories have come out over the past few years about major banks, companies, and other agencies having their information hacked and the potential for identity theft is higher than ever as a result. When using Bitcoin, identity theft is almost impossible. Your public address is visible, but your public address is simply a randomly generated string of numbers and letters, with no actual identifying information. As we discussed, skilled computer programmers may be able to gather information about you, but not the kind of information needed to steal your identity or your money.

The main obstacles to using technology such as Bitcoin is the acceptance of others; all monetary or currency systems only work if most everyone agrees to use it. The more people, organizations, and countries that accept Bitcoin and other cryptocurrencies as valid, the more potent and stable bitcoins become. Because this acceptance is still in its early phases, small changes or transactions in the world of Bitcoin can affect its value and cause more dramatic ebbs and flows than would happen if it was more accepted. Experts argue that the more popular and widely used Bitcoin becomes, the less it will be affected by problems in one particular area. If the entire world had been using Bitcoin and the distribution of where bitcoins were stored was more diverse, the hack of Mt. Gox in 2014 would likely have not caused as much harm. It is likely that as more individuals get involved in using Bitcoin, the market will not experience such dramatic peaks and valleys.

As the public awareness of Bitcoin and blockchain has risen, thousands have flocked to the technology in hopes of making their fortune. Hundreds of technology whizzes are in pursuit of developing the next big cryptocurrency; most start by offering investors what's known as an initial coin offering, or I.C.O., in exchange for helping them get started. The SEC has promised to be harder on new companies starting out rather than established cryptocurrencies, as they fear that investors might be easily taken advantage of by con men. However, since Bitcoin has been around for a decade and is well-known, it is protected from the harsher regulations for newer cryptocurrencies. This protection, afforded in part by its notoriety, makes it an optimal choice for investing; especially in the United States, the government has made it clear that Bitcoin is welcome.

Universities are quickly catching on to the cryptocurrency craze and are helping to bring the blockchain into the mainstream by incorporating courses, interest groups, and initiatives directed at education and innovation. Duke University, long renowned as a leader in research, has established the Duke Blockchain Lab which is dedicated to educating Duke Students and faculty about the new world of cryptocurrency. Unsurprisingly, MIT is a leader in pushing for new research as well as developing guidelines for blockchain technologies. Cornell University, Georgetown University, and NYU are all working diligently on bringing education about cryptocurrency to the world. Stanford University, already known to be on the cutting edge of new technology, offers a course online about blockchain and cryptocurrency. NYU opened its first course on blockchain and cryptocurrency in 2014 and has continued to offer the course. The world of formal academia embracing this new movement is a vote of confidence for Bitcoin and its descendants. Universities have not only begun teaching about Bitcoin and blockchain, but some have also even started allowing students to pay their tuition using bitcoins. It's not only American institutions of higher learning that are taking note of Bitcoin and blockchain – Australia's Royal Melbourne Institute of Technology has also begun offering a short course in blockchain to help its students keep abreast of these new developments.

Despite the rises and falls in value, over the past 10 years, the overall rate has been a climb in value for Bitcoin. When it was initially launched, a bitcoin was worth just pennies; at the time of this writing, one Bitcoin is valued at over $6,000. Ignoring the hysteria both for and against Bitcoin, this dramatic increase in value speaks for itself. While some critics don't see a future for Bitcoin, you have to remember that for the ten years of its existence these same critics have been foretelling Bitcoin's demise, and at present, it doesn't show any sign of slowing down. Bitcoin is like Rocky – no matter how many times it gets knocked down or how broken it seems to be, it always seems to find a way to rise again. Many experts believe that there has never been a better time to take the leap into the world of cryptocurrency, and there's no better virtual currency to do that with than the original Bitcoin.

Conclusion

Congratulations, you are ready to step out into the world, armed with your new knowledge about Bitcoin! You've lived through the life journey of Bitcoin, and now you have an understanding of the processes that operate behind the scenes as well as the groups of people who have made the birth of Bitcoin possible. You know now that despite its up and downs, Bitcoin is likely to be around for years to come, and now is the perfect time to get invested in the founding cryptocurrency.

The next step is to decide for yourself whether you are ready to take the leap into Bitcoin, and if so, find someone to buy from and get started! Do your research on what kind of Bitcoin wallet will work best for you and whether or not you want to use a web-based coin exchange, keeping in mind that using an exchange will make your bitcoins less secure. Explore other cryptocurrencies and see if there are any others that you might want to invest in as well, and keep an eye on the market. Connect with other people who are interested in Bitcoin and find family members or friends who might want to invest with you — you might be surprised who else is investing in Bitcoin. Finally, remember that Bitcoin is still young, and don't be alarmed by every rise and fall in the price — Bitcoin has experienced dramatic fluctuations in price over the years, but the overall direction has been a steady rise in value.

Finally, if you found this book useful in any way, a review on Amazon is always appreciated!

Description

Have you ever wondered what this 'Bitcoin' craze is all about? What is a cryptocurrency, really? Is it something that you should be interested in or know anything about, or is it another fad that will be gone in a few years? In this book, you will have all these questions – and more – answered. Are you ready to be able to talk about cryptocurrency like you really understand it? You're in the right place. Learn more about how Bitcoin is changing the future and the world of money altogether so that you can make an educated decision about your own investments.

In this book, we will explore
- the mysterious origins of Bitcoin and its creator
- the massive benefits that one can gain from using a cryptocurrency
- the ways that Bitcoin works to ensure security and privacy in a digital age
- how Bitcoin will truly become the currency of the future

Did you know that a U.S. Senator has invested in Bitcoin? Or that a failing country came to rely on Bitcoin to get essential items from all over the world? This book not only helps you to make educated choices about your financial future, but it also helps to give you some historical context for cryptocurrencies and to understand the reasons why the time was ripe for the emergence of Bitcoin.

In addition, we will provide a brief review of cryptocurrencies that are competing with Bitcoin, an easy to understand explanation of the technologies behind Bitcoin, and a nuanced look at the factors that helped make the rise of Bitcoin possible. We will look to the future and offer predictions of where Bitcoin will be in the future (hint: it's not slowing down any time soon!).

About the Author

Dan Wilson has extensive trading and financial experience. He is 34 years old, single, and lives in LA.

When he's not writing about Bitcoin, you can find him surfing, cooking, or spending time with his beloved dog.

www.ingramcontent.com/pod-product-compliance
Lightning Source LLC
Chambersburg PA
CBHW030455220526
45464CB00006B/2545